To:

From:

A pocket guide to

he's just not that into you

that into you

The No-Excuses Truth to
Understanding Guys

greg behrendt
and
liz tuccillo

Peter Pauper Press, Inc.
White Plains, New York

The text in this book is excerpted from
*He's Just Not That Into You: The No-Excuses Truth to
Understanding Guys* by Greg Behrendt and
Liz Tuccillo, originally published by Simon Spotlight
Entertainment in 2004. Text copyright © 2004
by Greg Behrendt and Liz Tuccillo.
All rights reserved.

Designed by Karine Syvertsen

Published in 2005 by arrangement with
Simon Spotlight Entertainment, an imprint of
Simon & Schuster, Inc.

Peter Pauper Press, Inc.
202 Mamaroneck Avenue
White Plains, NY 10601
All rights reserved
ISBN 1-59359-990-0
Printed in China
7 6 5 4 3 2

Visit us at www.peterpauper.com

the no-excuses truth to
understanding guys

he's just **not**
that into you

Contents

Introduction by Liz

I t started out just like any other day. We were all working in the writers' room of *Sex and the City* talking, pitching ideas, our personal love lives weaving in and out of the fictional lives we were creating in the room. And just like on any other day, one of the women on staff asked for feedback on the behavior of a man whom she liked. He was giving her mixed messages— she was confused. . . . And just like on any other day, after much analysis and debate, we concluded that she was *fabulous,* he must be scared, he's never met a woman as great as her, he is intimidated, and she should just give him time. But on this day, we had a male consultant in the room—someone who comes in a couple of times a week to give feedback on story lines and gives a great straight-male perspective: Greg Behrendt. On this day, Greg listened intently to the story and our reactions, and then said to the woman in question, "Listen, it sounds like he's just not that into you."

Now, at first glance it seems that this should have been demoralizing to us. . . . Yet the opposite was true. Knowledge is power, and more importantly, knowledge saves us time. . . . Greg reminded us that we were all beautiful, smart, funny women, and we shouldn't be wasting our time figuring out why a guy isn't calling us. As Greg put it, we shouldn't waste the pretty.

It's hard. . . . We go out with someone, we get excited about them, and then they do something that mildly disappoints us. . . . We try to come up with some explanation for why they're behaving that way, any explanation . . . than the one explanation that's the truth: He's just not that into me.

That's why we've included questions from women taken from real situations. . . . So read, enjoy, and hopefully learn from other women's confusion. And above all, if the guy you're dating doesn't seem to be completely into you, or you feel the need to start "figuring him out," please consider the glorious thought that he might just not be that into you. And then free yourself to go find the one that is.

So I'm sitting in the writers' room at *Sex and the City* pondering my good fortune to be the only straight male on the predominantly female writing staff (actually I'm just eating a cookie), when the writers begin talking about guys they're seeing.

So on this particular day, one of the ladies pipes up with "Greg, you're a guy." She is very observant, this one, for I am indeed a guy. Then she says, "So I've been seeing this guy. . . . Well, I think I have." I know the answer. "See, we went to a movie and it was great. I mean he didn't hold my hand, but that's cool. I don't like to hold hands." Still know the answer. "But afterward he kissed me in the parking lot. So I asked if he wanted to come over, but he had a really important meeting in the morning so he didn't come over." C'mon. Are you kidding me? Know it!

So I asked, "Have you heard from him?"

"Well, that's the thing. This was like a week ago"—now *you* should know the answer—"and then today he e-mails me and is like, 'Why haven't I heard from you?'"

This superstar of a woman is confused about a situation that to me is so clear. Actually, confused is the wrong word.... She's hopeful, not confused. But the situation is hopeless, so I broke the news to her: "He's just not that into you."

Men are not complicated, although we'd like you to think we are, as in "Things are really crazy right now. I've just got a ton of shit going on." We are driven by sex, although we'd like to pretend otherwise.... If a dude isn't calling you when he says he will, or making sure you know that he's dating you, then you already have your answer. Stop making excuses for him, his actions are screaming the truth: He's just not that into you.

You know you deserve to have a great relationship. We agree. So grab a highlighter and get started. Liz told you I was going to say it: Don't waste the pretty!

he's just not that into you if he's not asking you out

Because if he likes you, trust me, he will ask you out

M en find it very satisfying to get what they want. . . . If we want you, we will find you.

We have put the stories we have

heard and questions we've been asked in a simple question-and-answer format. If you're lucky, you'll read the following questions and know what they are: Excuses that women have made for their unsatisfying situations. If you're not so lucky, we've also included handy titles to clue you in.

The "But He Gave Me His Number" Excuse

Dear Greg,
I met a really cute guy at a bar. . . . He gave me his number. . . . I thought that was kind

of cool, that he gave me control of the situation like that. I can call him, right?
Lauren

Dear Control Freak,
Did he give you control, or did he just get you to do the heavy lifting? What he just did was a magic trick. . . . Why don't you take Copperfield's number, roll it in a newspaper, pour milk in it, and make it disappear.

Men, for the most part, like to pursue women. We like not knowing if we can catch you. We feel rewarded when we do. Especially when the chase is a long one.

! IT'S SO SIMPLE

"Please, if you can trust one thing I say in this book, let it be this: *When it comes to men, deal with us as we are, not how you'd like us to be.*" . . . My belief is that if you have to be the aggressor . . . he's just not that into you. . . . I can't say it loud enough: You, the superfox reading this book, are worth asking out.

HERE'S WHY THIS ONE IS HARD, by Liz

Most women who date, I would guess, don't have men throwing themselves at them every night of the week. Sometimes there's a long stretch during which nobody's asking us out. So when we see a guy that we feel might be a romantic possibility, it's even harder for us to take a backseat.

But guess what: My way? Has sucked. Hasn't worked at all. I've never had a successful relationship with a guy that I've pursued.

Since I've been implementing

Greg's handy-dandy "he's just not that into you" philosophy, I've been feeling surprisingly *more* powerful. . . . And most importantly, it's good for us all to remember that we don't need to scheme and plot and beg to get someone to ask us out. We're fantastic.

THIS IS WHAT IT SHOULD LOOK LIKE, by Greg

An actor we work with met a girl while he was making a public appearance on an aircraft carrier. He lost track of her in about ten minutes. And yet, because he was so smitten, he somehow managed to track her down in the army, and they are now married.

What You Should Have Learned in This Chapter

✓ Don't get tricked into asking him out. If he likes you, he'll do the asking.

✓ If he wants to find you, he will.

✓ You are good enough to be asked out.

he's just not that into you if he's not calling you

Men know how to use the phone

With the advent of cell phones and speed dialing it is almost impossible *not* to call you. Sometimes I call people from my pants pocket when

I don't even mean to. . . . If I were into you, you would be the bright spot in my horribly busy day. Which would be a day that I would never be too busy to call you.

Yes, it seems like it's just a machine that transmits voice waves over wires and comes in different styles . . . but the truth is, the phone has officially reached a new high in relationship symbolism. . . . And a good man will know that and use this handy telecommunication device accordingly. E-mails need not apply.

THIS IS WHAT IT SHOULD LOOK LIKE, by Liz

When I was working with Greg on this book in New York, I noticed that Greg would often call his wife just to tell her that he couldn't really talk to her right then, but he was thinking of her and would call later. It didn't look like the most difficult thing in the world, but it sure seemed nice.

GREG, I GET IT! By Traci, age 25

Greg, I get it! I had two dates with a guy. On the second date we slept together. He said he would call me the next day (Tuesday) and he didn't call me until the weekend. When he called, I told him that it was too late. . . . I don't have time for that shit. It was the first time I had ever done anything like that and it felt great!

What You Should Have Learned in This Chapter

✓ If he's not calling you, it's because you are not on his mind.

✓ "Busy" is another word for "asshole." "Asshole" is another word for the guy you're dating.

✓ You deserve a f-cking phone call.

he's just not that into you if he's not dating you

"Hanging out" is not dating

Oh, there seem to be so many variations to dating, particularly in the early stages of a relationship. So many gray, murky areas of vagueness, mystery, and no questions asked.

Dudes love this time because that's when they get to pretend they're not really dating you. Then they also get to pretend they're not really responsible for your feelings.

The "It's Better Than Nothing" Excuse

Dear Greg,

I've been dating a guy for six months. We see each other about every two weeks. We have a great time, we have sex, it's all really nice. I thought if I just let things develop, we would start to see each other more often. . . . I really like him, so I still feel like it's better than nothing. . . . I know he's really busy . . . So maybe I should actually feel honored that he's able to give me as much time as he does . . . No?

Lydia

Dear Better Than Nothing,

Really? Is better than nothing what we're going for now? . . . Why should you feel honored for getting scraps of his time? Just because he's busy doesn't make him more valuable. "Busy" does not mean "better." In my book, any guy who can wait two weeks to see you, is just not that into you.

! IT'S SO SIMPLE

From this moment on, right now, as you read this, make this solemn vow about your future romantic relationships: no more murky, no more gray, no more unidentified, and no more undeclared. And if at all possible, try to know someone as best you can before you get naked with them.

What You Should Have Learned in This Chapter

✓ "I don't want to be in a serious relationship" truly means "I don't want to be in a serious relationship with you" or "I'm not sure that you're the one." (Sorry.)

✓ Better than nothing is not good enough for you!

✓ Murky? Not good.

4

he's just not that
into you if he's
having sex with
someone else

*There's never going to be a
good excuse for cheating*

The "But I've Gotten Fat" Excuse

Dear Greg,

I had been dating a guy for about two years . . . After he came home from a family visit, he told me he slept with someone he met at a bar. . . . He told me I had put on some weight and therefore he wasn't that attracted to me anymore. . . . I have put on about twenty pounds. Should I break up with him or start going to the gym?

Beth

Dear Twenty Pounds,

I definitely think you should lose 175 pounds—in the form of your loser boyfriend—not the twenty that you're talking about. He just cheated on you and called you fat. . . . Get rid of this loser or I'm going to come to your house and get rid of him for you.

💡 GREG, I GET IT! By Adele, age 26

I was dating a guy I really liked who played in a popular local band. After a few weeks

Sometimes all the psychological help in the world can't do anything. Sometimes boredom just has to set in. You get bored with always having less than everybody else seems to have, less than what you want. You start thinking that maybe you actually deserve better. . . . That's what happened to me, I think. I hope it will be a lot faster for you.

💡 GREG, I GET IT! By Janine, age 43

I recently met a guy online whose wife had passed away three months earlier. We went out a few times and it was clear he wasn't really ready to be dating. . . . I told him I didn't feel comfortable dating him so soon after his wife's death, but that I hadn't closed any doors, and would love to see him again when more time had passed. Then I went back online and continued my search.

What You Should Have Learned in This Chapter

✓ Unless he's all yours, he's still hers.

✓ There are cool, loving *single* men in the world. Find one of them to go out with.

✓ He's married.

✓ Don't be that girl.

List all the things you want or have ever wanted in a man. We'll give you five lines. We'll wait. . . .

1.

2.

3.

4.

5.

Now look at your list. Did "married" or "emotionally unavailable" make that list? Yeah, we didn't think so. You're far too classy and smart for that.

he's just not that into you if he's a selfish jerk, a bully, or a really big freak

If you really love someone, you want to do things to make that person happy

If you date, you will meet your share of weirdos and jerks. That is as sure as death and taxes. The only thing in your control is how long you allow these gentlemen to take up space in your life.

HERE'S WHY THIS ONE IS HARD, by Liz

I've been implying this in my "Here's Why This One Is Hard" responses, but now I'm just going to come right out with it: There aren't that many good men around. Statistics prove it, articles and books have been written to verify it, and women would be happy to testify under oath about it.

I know we have to love ourselves and think we deserve happiness and be optimistic. I also think it sucks to be single. Greg, are you really telling us that we should just stay single and picky and not settle (and thus not settle down) until we have met the person we think is the one? It's really lonely out there. You take this one. I don't have a clue.

Being lonely, being alone, for many people, sucks. I get it, I get it, I get it. But still I have to say that, yes, my true belief is that being with somebody who makes you feel shitty or doesn't honor the person you are, is worse.

The statistics are bleak. But don't use statistics to keep you down or keep you frightened. You can't do anything with these statistics except scare yourself and your girlfriends. So I say, "F-ck statistics." It's your life— how dare you not have faith in it!

You are delicious. Be brave, my sweet. I know you can get lonely. I know you can crave companionship and sex and love so badly that it physically hurts. But I truly believe that the only way you can find out that there's something better out there is to first *believe* there's something better out there. I'll believe it for you until you're ready.

What You Should Have Learned in This Chapter

✓ You deserve to be with someone who is nice to you all the time.

✓ Freaks should remain at the circus, not in your apartment.

✓ Make a space in your life for the glorious things you deserve.

✓ Have faith. What other choice is there?

now what do you do?

*n*ow, there's a million things you can do after a breakup ... The first thing we're going to recommend is setting some standards.

STANDARD SUGGESTIONS

- I will not go out with a man who hasn't asked me out first.

- I will not go out with a man who keeps me waiting by the phone.

- I will not date a man who isn't sure he wants to date me.

- I will not date a man who makes me feel sexually undesirable.

- I will not date a man who drinks or does drugs to an extent that makes me uncomfortable.

- I will not be with a man who's afraid to talk about our future.

- I will not, under any circumstances, spend my precious time with a man who has already rejected me.

- I will not date a man who is married.

- I will not be with a man who is not clearly a good, kind, loving person.

Now it's your turn. Only you know the standards you haven't set for yourself. Write them down. Don't forget them.

closing remarks from greg

Don't waste the pretty

I t's all fun and games to have some insight and a witty reply to your letters, but at the core the "He's just not that into you" concept can truly have a magical transcendent effect. It's not bad news if it helps you free yourself from a relationship that is beneath you. And we both know that only you can free yourself. I don't pretend to know how to fix you. I do know how to help you recognize the problem. I do know that you are worthy of having great relationships and an even better life. I do think you are beautiful and somewhere deep down inside you know it too, otherwise you wouldn't be here. I believe life is a speedy and awesome gift, so don't waste the pretty. If you are reading this, *you* want something better. If you are reading this, I want something better for you too.

—Greg

of dating he told me that he slept with some girl after one of his gigs. Sadly, a few years ago I probably would have been so into dating a guy in a band that I would have just pretended it had never happened and forgotten he had ever told me about it. This time, I told him that it was cool; he's allowed to do whatever he wants. He just won't be seeing me ever again. It felt great!

What You Should Have Learned in This Chapter

✓ There is no excuse for cheating. Let me say it again. There is no excuse for cheating. Now you say it. There is no excuse for cheating.

✓ Cheaters never prosper. (Because they suck.)

✓ A cheater only cheats himself, because he doesn't get to be with *you*.

he's just not that into you if he only wants to see you when he's drunk

If he likes you, he'll want to see you when his judgment isn't impaired

The "But I Like Him This Way" Excuse

Dear Greg,

My boyfriend . . . really likes to drink. . . . And when he's drunk he's really affection- ate and tells me all these great things about how he feels about me. . . . He doesn't miss work. He's just a bad boy. I like bad boys. They're exciting. If you don't, you're too uptight.

Nikki

Dear Nikki,

You can't believe everything a guy says when he's drunk. And take it from a former bad boy: "Bad Boys" are bad because they're troubled, as in having little self-respect, lots of pent-up anger, loads of self-loathing, complete lack of faith in any kind of loving relationship, but yes, really cool clothes and often a great car. Just the kind of guy for you, right, Nikki?

 HERE'S WHY THIS ONE IS HARD, by Liz

So what's hard about this one? Nothing much. Except, boy, does alcohol factor in a lot in the beginning stages of dating. The first kiss, the first time having sex . . . most relationships would never get off the ground without a couple of glasses of wine first, and there ain't nothing wrong with that.

So we all have to be clear about the difference between a couple of drinks to relax, and constant substance abuse. Okay. Got it.

What You Should Have Learned in This Chapter

✓ Drinking and drug use are not a path to one's innermost feelings.

✓ Bad boys are actually bad.

✓ You deserve to be with someone who doesn't have to get loaded to be around you.

6

he's just not that into you if he doesn't want to marry you

Love cures commitment-phobia

There is nothing wrong with wanting to get married. You shouldn't feel ashamed, needy, or "unliberated" for wanting that.

The "Is This Really an Excuse?" Dilemma

Dear Greg,

I'm thirty-three and have been living with a guy for two years. We are in love, he's great to me, and we get along perfectly. . . . He married young and got divorced young. He says he doesn't want to ruin a good thing. . . . He's even open to having kids. . . . In this case, I don't think he's just not that into me. I think he's just not that into marriage.

Lindsey

Dear Common Law Lady,

Only you can decide if marriage is a deal breaker for you. I can't tell you if it's worth breaking up with him if you're happy and have a nice life together. . . . I have never been divorced, I'll give you that, but I'd marry my wife in every time zone if that's what she wanted.

HERE'S WHY THIS ONE IS HARD, by Liz

A lot of people think marriage is bull-shit. A lot of women, men, philosophers, anthropologists, psychologists, feminists, and scientists all think, for different reasons, that marriage is a deeply flawed, outdated institution built for failure.

The question at hand is only this: Is he making lame transparent excuses about marriage to cover for the fact that he really doesn't ever see a future with you?

What You Should Have Learned in This Chapter

✓ "Doesn't want to get married" and "Doesn't want to get married to me" are very different things.

✓ If you have different views about marriage, what else are you not on the same page about?

✓ There's a guy out there who wants to marry you.

he's just not that into you if he's breaking up with you

"I don't want to go out with you" means just that

What could be better than hearing from the man who just told you he didn't want you in his life any-more, his sad, wistful "I miss you so much" voice on the other end of the phone?

Don't be flattered that he misses you. He *should* miss you. You're deeply missable. However, he's still the same person who just broke up with you.

The "But Everyone Is Doing It" Excuse

Dear Greg,
Yes. Breakup sex. It's been hot. Emotional. Amazing. I'm tortured and I love him and

I can't stop myself. I thought that you were allowed breakup sex, but now I'm in over my head. Help.
Ileen

Dear If You Know Better, Why Are You Still at His Apartment?
Hey, girl. Put down the penis, put your clothes back on, and go directly to your best friend's house. . . . He's not into you.

49

Breaking up means not seeing them again, which also implies not seeing them naked again.

👥 THIS IS WHAT IT SHOULD LOOK LIKE, by Liz

I know a couple who dated for many years and then broke up. . . . Five years later, they got back together again and are now happily married. During the time apart, there were no dates or phone calls or being chums. . . . They moved on with their lives, grew up separately, and only then realized, much later, that they could be together again.

What You Should Have Learned in This Chapter

✓ You can't talk your way out of a breakup. It is not up for discussion.

✓ Breakup sex still means you're broken up.

✓ Cut him off. Let him miss you.

he's just not that into you if he's disappeared on you

Sometimes you have to get closure all by yourself

He's gone. Poof. Vanished into thin air. Well, there's no mixed message here. . . . It's so painful, it's impossible not to be hurt or angry. But

because of that, you might be tempted to make some excuses for yourself. . . . But all those excuses, however valid they are, will not help you in the long run.

The "But Can't I at Least Yell at Him" Excuse?

Dear Greg,

I was dating a guy seriously for three months when he suddenly disappeared. . . . I get that he's just not that into me, but don't I have the right to find out how he could do that to me? Don't I have the right to not let him get away with it?

Renee

Dear Just Walk Away Renee,

Sure. But guess what. He knows you're going to be pissed. He's a colossal asshole, not an idiot. He played the whole thing out in his head. That's why he just disappeared.

P.S.: And he's not getting away with anything. Everywhere he goes, he's still that same asshole.

In the short term it might feel good to call someone and yell at him. But in the long run, you will have wished that you had not given him that much credit for ruining your life. Or even your day. Let someone else expend that kind of energy on him.

❗ IT'S SO SIMPLE

Don't ask yourself what you did wrong or how you could have done it differently. Don't waste your valuable heart and mind trying to figure out why he did what he did. . . . The only thing you need to know is that it's really good news: He's gone. Hallelujah.

HERE'S WHY THIS ONE IS HARD, by Liz

Oh, for Pete's sake. This one is *impossible*. He *disappeared*. He just stopped calling you or writing you or seeing you *out of the blue*. You were in what you considered some sort of "relationship." You felt that whatever you had together warranted even the tiniest explanation if one of you decided to call it quits. But instead, there's silence. No explanation, no good-bye. Just a vanishing. There's nothing worse, in dating terms, *nothing worse*, than that sick feeling you get in the pit of your stomach when it looks like the guy you were seeing or getting to know has decided to bail on you instead of talking to you about it.

But I guess the hope is (for me, at least) that when a guy no longer wants to communicate with me, and doesn't have the manners or courage to tell me that to my face, he's given me all the information I need. It's the toughest one of all to put into practice. But I definitely like the kind of girl who could do it. Good luck to us all!

What You Should Have Learned in This Chapter

✓ No answer is your answer.

✓ Don't give him the chance to reject you again.

✓ Let his mother yell at him. You're too busy.

✓ There's no mystery—he's gone and he wasn't good enough for you.

he's just not that into you if he's married (and other insane variations of being unavailable)

If you're not able to love freely, it's not really love

Ifthe person you "love" (notice the snotty quotation marks around that) cannot freely spend his days thinking about you and being with you, *it's not real love.*

The "But He's Really a Good Person" Excuse

Dear Greg,
I never thought I'd be in this situation. I know you're not supposed to date married men, but here I am. . . . We are deeply in love. I'm thirty-six years old and I have never in my life felt anything this powerful

before. . . . He talks about leaving his wife, but he has two young children, and this would be devastating to them. . . . I feel awful, and yet I also believe I deserve to feel this kind of love.

Belinda

Dear Other Woman,

Hey, smart girl. Good for you to know you deserve to feel a powerful and profound love. I just think you should have it with someone who's actually *yours*.

! IT'S SO SIMPLE

Yes. You are going to meet many men in many different stages of recovering from relationships. If he is really into you, he will get over his issues fast and make sure he doesn't lose you.

HERE'S WHY THIS ONE IS HARD, by Liz

Because it's you—not someone you read about or heard about or saw on TV. It's you and it's hard. And you deserve happiness just like his wife or his girlfriend does.

closing remarks from liz

Greg can be really annoying

reg can be really annoying. I understand. I work with him. Even during the writing of this book he has managed to dash my hopes and dreams about men I have been optimistic about dating. It seems no one is good enough for Greg.

But I do think he's right—a lot of the time—which is the most annoying part of it all. Greg is the older brother we all should have in our lives (and in our heads). He demands that men treat us better than even we think they should.

I hope this book was helpful to you. I hope it made you laugh a little, in recognition. And I hope you find fantastic, healthy, life-changing love, just the way you had imagined it.

With perhaps a few surprises thrown in just for fun.

—Liz